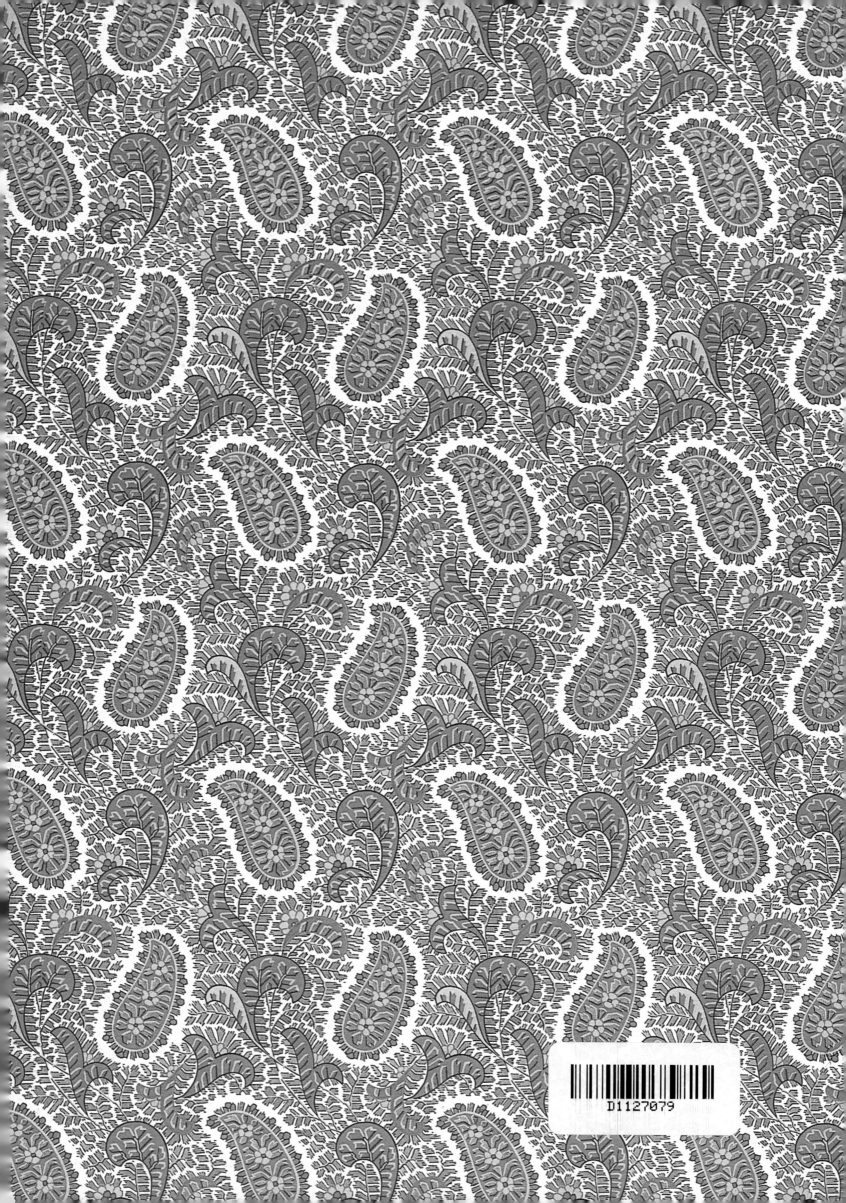

D1127079

Paisley Patterns

PAISLEY
PATTERNS

A DESIGN SOURCE BOOK

by

Valerie Reilly

Keeper of Textiles and Local History
The Paisley Museum and Art Gallery, Scotland

PORTLAND HOUSE
NEW YORK

Published by Portland House
a division of dilithium Press, Ltd.
Distributed by Crown Publishers, Inc.
225 Park Avenue South
New York New York 10003

Paisley Patterns *contains a selection*
of designs from the Paisley Museum
and Art Gallery, Scotland

ISBN 0-517-69261-9

Printed in Malaysia

h g f e d c b a

Introduction

A pattern which unites the cultures of the eastern and western hemispheres is known in the English language as the Paisley Pattern. But how many people question the way in which such an obviously exotic, oriental pattern came to be connected with a small Scottish textile town? Of course the pattern did not originate there, but today half the world would recognize the motif as a 'Paisley', even if they had not the remotest idea where the place itself lay. The story behind that connection is a long and convoluted one, and perhaps one of the strangest tales in the field of textile design.

The origins of the motif can be found in the ancient civilization of Babylon under the rule of kings such as Nebuchadnezzar. There, one of the predominant food sources was the date palm. However, the tree was not important for food alone; it also provided building materials, such as wood, string and thatch. So as a supply of both food and shelter, the two main necessities of life, the date palm came to be seen as the Tree of Life. It is thought that the motif itself is a representation of the tightly curled palm frond just as it begins to grow. As such, it was a symbol of fertility, and probably all the more prized by the Babylonians on that account. From Babylon the use of the motif spread throughout the civilized world. In Europe the motif was taken over by the Celtic peoples and its descent can easily be seen in the curves and swirls of their art. Under the Greek and, later, the Roman empires, however, the dominant art-forms were more representational. The Celts were pushed to the very fringes of the European continent and their arts largely disregarded.

In contrast the peoples of the Asian continent, particularly in India, continued to use the Babylonian motif in many media from stonecarving to textiles. Recent research in America seems to indicate that it first appeared on shawls in India at some time during the 1600s, but the earliest examples are known only from the miniature paintings of nobles, princes and holy men. Probably the oldest surviving shawl, or rather two fragments of it known to be in different museums, is dated about 1680 and consists of single plant forms spaced over the end borders of a rectangle of cream pashmina (best goat's hair fibre). But those single plant forms, on closer examination, can be seen to be constrained within the outline shape we recognize today as 'Paisley' – a kind of teardrop turned to one side at the top.

The process of transferring the motif onto one of these early shawls was both complicated and laborious. The pattern-drawer produced the original design and was the most highly paid of the Kashmiri shawl workers. Working from his black and white design, the colour-caller specified the colour of yarn to be used and the number of warp threads to be covered. This was noted down in a kind of shorthand by the pattern-master. The warps were set up on frame looms by groups of specialists and then handed over to the weavers. Instead of throwing a shuttle from one side of the loom to the other, the weaver worked with between 400 and 1,500 spools to weave each patch of colour into the design separately. This is weaving by what is known as the twill-tapestry technique. It was extremely time-consuming: one single shawl could take up to a year and a half to complete.

The material of which the best shawls were made was goat hair. A species of wild goat, that lived high in the Himalayas, each winter grew a downy underfleece to protect it from the intense cold. During the subsequent spring that fine hair would be shed onto the rocks and bushes whence it could be gathered for cleaning and spinning. Obviously there was only a limited supply of this wild goat hair, or pashmina, and domesticated goats never seemed to produce a fleece of equivalent fineness. The best shawls therefore were always a scarce commodity, and in Kashmir, where they were a man's garment, they were so highly regarded that they were often presented as gifts between princes.

The first Europeans to take an interest in the shawls were the men of the British East India Company. During the middle years of the eighteenth century they began to include a few shawls amongst the gifts they brought back to their womenfolk. These first shawls were greatly admired on the British fashion scene, and before long the Company found that they were very much in demand. What had started out as a casual gift soon became a serious commercial import. One problem still remained, however: shawls were scarce, and by the time they reached Britain they would cost the fashionable lady who wished to acquire one between £200 and £300. Obviously only the social élite could afford to own a Kashmir shawl.

Because of the demand for shawls, British manufacturers began to investigate ways of imitating the imports from Kashmir. The first centre to produce imitation shawls, however, was not Paisley. Edinburgh trade records show that shawls 'in imitation of the Indian', as they were termed, were being woven from 1777. Another weaving centre to join the trade was Norwich, which began making shawls in 1784. Paisley, however, was at this time famed for the quality of the silk it produced and had no need to take up a new and as yet untried product.

So how did Paisley become involved in the shawl trade, and, even more interestingly, become a world leader in shawl manufacture? Perhaps the blame can be laid at the door of Revolutionary France and Napoleon Bonaparte. The wars with France had drained British resources, and attempts to beat the French navy's blockade were confined to more essential imports than raw silk. As a result many of the very highly skilled weavers in Paisley found themselves without work in the early years of the nineteenth century. Manufacturers in the town were desperate to find a new product which could revive the weaving trade. In around 1805, so the story goes, an Edinburgh shawl manufacturer by the name of Paterson had taken on too many orders for shawls. His own weavers were unable to match the demand; so, remembering the pool of skilled weavers in Paisley, he sent them some work. The Paisley workers soon realized that good profits could be made from shawl weaving, and before long several had set themselves up as shawl manufacturers.

Though first introduced some thirty years previously, the British shawls were still fashionable. In fact they were to remain part of the fashion-conscious woman's wardrobe for the best part of a century. This was due in no small measure to their versatility. Not only could the colours and designs be changed to suit the tastes of the age, but also the actual size and shape of the shawl could be adapted to suit the garment worn beneath.

The costumes of the early years of the nineteenth century were based on classical Graeco-Roman lines. Sleeves were tight-fitting, the dresses fell from beneath the bust and skirts were straight.

The lines of the costumes were extremely severe, and so the softness of the draped shawl, combined with the touch of the exotic in the pattern, provided the perfect complement. By the 1820s a change had occurred in dress design. The 'waistline' had dropped to something like its actual anatomical level, skirts had begun to flare out slightly, and the shoulder-line was greatly emphasized. The leg-o'-mutton sleeve had arrived. In response to this trend, the shawl changed in shape from a rectangle to a square. Folded across the diagonal, and worn around the shoulders to accentuate their width, with the point of the triangle highlighting the narrow waist, the shawl again proved to be an ideal accessory.

The next major change in style came in the 1840s with the gradual development of the crinoline. The ever increasing width of skirts made it difficult to wear a coat. Shawls responded by reverting to the rectangular shape but were some 50 per cent larger than they had been previously. Folded in half to conceal the 'wrong' side and adjusted for length, the big plaids (as these later rectangles were termed) could be draped around the wearer to form the equivalent of an outdoor coat. In this way the shawl again made itself indispensable to the fashionable lady. It was only when the bustle came into fashion in the 1870s that shawls were replaced by the short jackets and capes which were better suited to revealing the glories of the new skirts. Shawls and plaids were carefully put away in wardrobes and chests in the hope that the fashion for wearing them would soon be revived. As outer garments, of course, they never returned to general use but instead became family heirlooms to be cherished, and in some instances brought out for special occasions, particularly Christenings. In this way they have survived until the present day, when once again the mastery of the weaving techniques, together with the splendour and variety of the patterns, are fully appreciated.

As with the industry in Kashmir, the manufacture of shawls in Paisley was a complicated process. To produce shawls cheaply enough to compete with the imports from Kashmir, European weavers had to employ the technology with which they were familiar, rather than try to learn the complex twill-tapestry technique. In the early years of the nineteenth century they used the drawloom, since it was the only available apparatus that was capable of producing a pattern with curved lines. However, it was somewhat limited, since the 'flower-lashing' (or tying of the harness) put an effective restriction on the complexity of the repeat that could be produced. In addition, a drawloom required two operatives, the weaver himself and a youngster called the drawboy, whose job it was to pull the simples hanging down the side of the loom. This process raised the correct harness cords, allowing the weaver to put through a coloured weft thread according to the design being woven. Thus, when the Jacquard loom began to be introduced in large numbers in the 1840s, not only did the weaving become a one-man operation, but, since the weft threads were controlled by individual pattern cards, the variation in the pattern could be almost infinite.

The weaver and his drawboy were only one link in the chain of production. One of the reasons why Paisley's industry outstripped that of the other production centres was its efficient division of labour. It was reckoned that some eleven different specialists had a hand in the manufacture of each typical Paisley shawl. Yarns imported from the West Riding of Yorkshire were prepared by very highly skilled dyers; a beamer would measure out the warp threads and a warper would take over the task of entering them into the loom. Even the weaver's wife had a job to do. Using a simple winding wheel she would put the weft threads onto the pirns or bobbins ready to fit into the shuttles. After the weaver had finished, the shawls were taken to the manufacturer's warehouse for finishing. Firstly, the shawl would be passed beneath the revolving blades of the cropping machine. This removed, from the reverse side, all the surplus floating weft threads created by a weaving process that bore more than a passing resemblance to Fair Isle knitting. Next, the shawls would be washed, and then stretched over huge frames to dry evenly. Teams of girls were employed either to sew on pre-manufactured fringes, or to twist the warp thread-ends to form the fringing. Finally, the shawls were calendered, or steam-pressed, to give a wonderful sheen to the surface of the fabric. In fact this finish was so popular that some manufacturers would re-calender shawls for their customers.

By far the longest and most painstaking process in the production of a Paisley shawl, however, was the design stage, which is said to have taken up four-fifths of the total production time. The manufacturers obtained their designs from various sources. Other production centres continually accused Paisley of merely pirating designs that they had produced. But, to judge from the number of original pattern books in the collections of Paisley Museum, that can only be a small part of the whole picture. The government, however, considered the situation serious enough to allow, from 1842, the patenting of designs to protect them for periods of between three and twelve months. Records of these patents are lodged in the Record Office at Kew, and one or two of the pattern books at Paisley contain both the patent certificates and samples of the patterns they refer to.

As an alternative to what might today be called 'industrial espionage', the manufacturer had several options. He could buy in ready-made designs. We have evidence of this in Paisley in the form of numerous patterns stamped by designers in both London and Paris, the latter being considered perhaps more desirable by fashion-conscious customers. There also seem to have been freelance designers working in Paisley, selling individual patterns to interested shawl manufacturers. One of these was Thomas Holdway, originally a teacher of pattern design at the Edinburgh Art School. As the Edinburgh shawl industry weakened in the 1840s, he decided to move to the west of Scotland. A pattern class that he established in Glasgow seems to have failed, but sheets of pattern motifs signed by him exist in Paisley. In contrast, the largest manufacturers could, of course, afford to set up their own design studios with salaried employees.

For his initial inspiration, the working designer could choose from many sources. As has already been noted, Paisley was notorious for selling, naturally at a lower rate, copies of shawls from the other British weaving centres. Therefore it is likely that the manufacturers were buying new shawls as soon as they appeared. Perhaps this side of the business did not require the artistic skill of the designer, but it would certainly have needed the technical expertise of a draughtsman in order to produce the working drawings necessary to weave from. On the other hand, the manufacturers might have needed a designer to produce slight variations to the patterns, in order they they could truly say that their products were not just copies. Kashmir shawls were also bought directly from the importers and used to inspire new designs in Paisley. Another ready-made source of inspiration came in the form of books. These were often produced by the French and consisted of black and white drawings taken from existing shawls. One in particular, called *Le Cachemirien*, had drawings of Kashmir shawls belonging to the French nobility. And of course, as the Paisley shawl industry progressed, the designers could look back to the design books accumulating in the town and perhaps find inspiration there.

Whatever the source of the idea, the design process followed a well-established routine. First, the designer would get his idea down on paper in the form of a preliminary sketch. This was usually a black and white miniature of a half or a quarter of the finished pattern. The shawls were nearly always symmetrical, so from these sketches it was possible to get a picture of the whole design. Presumably these preliminary drafts were submitted to the manufacturer for initial approval. If this was received, then the designer would begin to work on coloured sketches of significant details within the design. These would include borders, corner motifs which fitted into plain centres, medallions and small sprigs to provide a filling for the background. Any, or all of these elements, could be combined to produce a new variety of shawl. Next, the complete colour scheme would be worked out, including the backgrounds. The preliminary sketches and coloured details were executed on ordinary paper, usually in white, though occasionally in black. The colour schemes, however, were put onto what was called oil-paper. This was specially treated to become nearly transparent, allowing the colourer to block in all the large areas of colour onto the back of the paper, so that the front was left free to paint in all the fiddly details without any fear of the colours running into one another. The final stage of the design sequence was to produce a working drawing, from which the loom could be set up to weave the desired pattern. For this part of the process use was made of point-paper, or weaver's graph paper, which was printed with squares of different sizes depending on the fineness of the weave. But printers in Paisley gave point-paper an extra refinement. As well as the usual squares, they also printed in the diagonals, as this helped to give the effect of the twill-weave in the finished patterns. It is unlikely that the designer himself would be involved at this stage. More probably the point-paper would be completed by a draughtsman, filling in the appropriate colours in each square by referring to the oil-paper, together with the designer's sketch and details. The finished point-paper, in which each small square represented one crossing of a warp and weft thread, was greatly enlarged compared to the size of the finished weaving. This was necessary because of the physical limitation on the size of paper square that could be coloured separately from the next, and then read off again by the flower-lasher, or card-cutter.

Of course, if the design were for a printed, rather than a woven shawl, then it would not be necessary to produce a point-paper. In this case the designer would produce finished artwork to show the effect of one printed block placed upon the plain material. From this the skilled block-cutter would be able to produce the correct outline of block, and within that outline, carve only the parts needed for each individual colour. He would thus end up with a set of perhaps five or six blocks, which were printed on top of each other to build up the complete image intended by the designer. A particular technique was used in the design of printed shawls, which were often required to imitate the woven shawls closely. This was to include, as an integral part of the design block, angled shading lines which, like the diagonals in the point-paper, were intended to give the effect of a twill-weave. In this case, however, they would actually appear in the piece of finished work.

It is of interest to consider how and where the Paisley designers received their training. Certainly, before the late 1840s there were no facilities within the town itself. To receive any kind of formal training in art they would have had either to travel daily to Glasgow, or to move away in order to attend an Art School such as that in Edinburgh. However, as the shawl industry prospered after 1845, manufacturers felt that it would be helpful if shawl designers could be trained nearer at hand. So, led by some of the largest amongst them, the manufacturers pressed the government to bring to Paisley one of the Schools of Design being set up across the country. This was agreed, and in 1848 the Government School of Design opened in Gilmour Street. Almost immediately, however, a clash occurred between the School and the leading manufacturers. Prominent amongst them was Mr Robert Kerr, perhaps the most important manufacturer of that period, who withdrew his support when he found that the students were spending their time drawing from classical sculptures. This, he felt, would make them 'good enough monumental masons', but not designers of shawls. Another opportunity for some form of further education came to Paisley at the same time, with the establishment of the Artisan's Institute in 1847. Perhaps those who attended the more practical, technical evening-classes held by the Institute were inspired to take their education even further and move on to the creative side of the shawl business; at all events, the School of Design flourished in Paisley, despite the initial problems, for a number of years, eventually being incorporated into a new technical college which was opened in the town late in the nineteenth century. There is now no higher level of art training available in Paisley, as this aspect of the college's functions was recently transferred to the Glasgow School of Art.

During its years of existence however, the School of Design sought to give its students an all-round education in art, and there is no doubt that they would have been exposed to the standard style manuals of the Victorian era. Whether these important works were of any great influence in the designing of shawls is difficult to tell, but in the few instances where we actually have a portfolio of one single designer's work, it becomes obvious that authorities such as Owen Jones were familiar and influential.

One thing that students would have to learn, either in the classroom or for themselves, was the effect of wearing the shawl. To see a full length 3m × 1.5m plaid exhibited as a flat work of art gives quite a different impression of its pattern from seeing it folded in half and draped around a lady's shoulders. The designer had to bear in mind all the time that the pattern would not be seen as it was on the paper in front of him. He had to allow for the way in which the shawl would be draped, in order that the design should be enhanced rather than concealed. Thus the big, heavy woollen plaids tend to have long motifs that stretch from shoulder level to ankle, taking the eye downwards with an almost gravitational force. The fine silk gauzes, however, usually had small repeating patterns which would not be obscured by the constant movement of the lightweight fabric.

The Paisley Museum collection is very rich in the pattern and sample books left behind by the shawl industry. It opened in

1871, as Scotland's very first municipally run museum, and did not immediately collect shawl-related items, even though the industry was in decline. Shawl-manufacture had been part of everyday life in Paisley for so long that it was not considered worthy of special attention. It was not until Glasgow held a big exhibition of shawls in 1902 that Paisley woke up to its heritage. An even bigger and better exhibition was held there in 1905. Fortunately, this was in time to catch the end of Paisley's textile industry which, even though it had given up shawl-weaving some thirty years previously, had hung on to many of the old pattern books. Inspired by the exhibition, many companies donated their books to the Museum. One or two firms hung on tenaciously right up to the early 1940s, but in most cases as they folded up, they followed the precedent of handing over their pattern books. So the collection shows virtually the whole spectrum of the Paisley Shawl industry, although it suffers a sad lack of very early material.

Some of the books contain samples of the woven or printed material and would have been kept in the manufacturer's warehouse, so that the customer could come in and be shown the range of current stock. Other books contain the designers' finished artwork. These were perhaps put together so that potential customers could pick out a shawl and commission its weaving. It certainly looks, from the way the books are set out, as if it was possible to choose from a range of borders and a range of centre patterns, which could be put together to form a 'custom-built' shawl. Some of the books are dated and have the name of the manufacturer, therefore giving the historian a useful tool in trying to date the more anonymous books. Other books are obviously 'scrap books'. It is difficult to tell whether these are genuine working books used in the industry, although we can be sure in one case that a particular book was put together by a devotee of the Paisley shawl as a representation of the best in Paisley design. Some of the books contain the oil-paper colour schemes as well as the paper designs. The oil-paper has now, however, become a museum curator's nightmare. Over the years, it has grown so brittle and cracked that it is threatening to break into small pieces. A much-needed programme of conservation was begun during 1988 as the result of a donation to the Museum by a commercial company making modern Paisley Shawls; it is hoped that this scheme will continue until all the paper designs have been conserved and remounted in new albums which will make them much more accessible to students and researchers.

The prospects of reproducing Paisley shawls in the traditional manner are somewhat more limited. Jacquard hand looms are few and far between; and, although Paisley Museum does own one that was originally used for shawl weaving, it was much modified in later years in order to weave coarser fabrics. Even more difficult to find today are people with the necessary skills and knowledge to work such a loom. Nothing daunted, during the quincentenary celebrations of the Burgh of Paisley in 1988, a project was initiated with a generous grant from the local Chamber of Commerce. A weaver trained by the Galashiels College of Textiles has been working at Paisley Museum over the past year on a dual project. Firstly he has been investigating the possibilities of returning the Museum's loom to its original state so that it would once more be capable of weaving a shawl. More importantly he has taken on the difficult task of researching the techniques of Paisley shawl-weaving. The weavers of the nineteenth century understood shawl-weaving so well, and believed everyone else understood it so well, that no-one ever troubled to write down a comprehensive account of the methods. All that has survived are generalized descriptions, vague hints and more detailed information on things that were unusual in shawl manufacture. Consequently it is proving a much longer task than originally anticipated to reach the stage of actual weaving. Nevertheless, it is hoped that within the foreseeable future, a shawl of a traditional design, probably a Kirking shawl with its limited colour combinations, will again be woven on a Jacquard hand loom in Paisley. Obviously this is in no way a commercial venture. The research stage has been very heavily subsidized, and it remains to be seen whether there will be a saleable product at the end. It is improbable therefore that any profit-making concern would be interested in such a costly project. One or two Jacquard woven shawls have appeared in the last couple of years, but they have neither the look nor the feel of the traditional article. The chances of a traditional type of shawl being viable are small, and it would not be likely to rival the technical mastery of the original shawls, which will no doubt continue to be appreciated.

The 'Paisley pattern' has already lasted for some 2,500 years and it is unlikely to disappear in a hurry. The Oriental peoples have always appreciated the beauty of the design, and it has also been taken to Western hearts since its introduction into Europe some 200 years ago. Fashions come and go, and very probably the current rage for Paisley will subside. But the pattern never completely fades away. Even when it is not high fashion, Paisley patterned items can be found along every High Street as a mainstay of classic men's attire. But nowhere is the heritage of the pattern more fully respected than in Paisley itself, where plans are in hand to set up a shawl study and research centre which will make access to the original designs and the actual textiles much easier for anyone with a genuine interest in the history of Paisley shawls.

When looking at the 150 individual patterns in this book (only a small selection from the whole collection), it is possible to trace many of the devices used by the designers when putting a Paisley shawl pattern together. In order to get the motifs to run with the lines of the weave, the designer would often construct a pencil grid within which he would draw. This can be seen particularly well in Plates 9 and 31. It is evident also in many of the other illustrations, but in Plate 56b it looks almost as if the pencil grid has influenced the geometric style of the pattern that has emerged. If a pattern consisted of a frequent repeat, then only one motif would be coloured in, but to give the idea of the repeat the next motif would be lightly pencilled into position as in Plates 15 and 16b. Plate 26 shows a similar characteristic: here only part of the border has been coloured in as against the much larger Paisley motif. Another way of saving time was to indicate only a few of the small sprigs that might fill the centre of a shawl. This method is evident in Plates 21, 27 and 25. Plate 62a (a design for a printed shawl) is similar, but also shows how only half of the large motifs needed to be filled in for the block-cutter to have all the details he required. Plate 87 is also for a printed shawl, but in this case it is the finished artwork for a block. The block would actually be cut with the little Paisley motif sticking out to one side so that the patterns could more easily be registered when placing the blocks onto the fabric. Sometimes the patterns in the books look only semi-finished as in Plate 81. It is possible that these rough sketches had some fault in them and were abandoned in favour of a better copy. Another device sometimes employed was to show how the primary motifs might look against different backgrounds, without doing separate drawings. This can be seen particularly well in Plate 25, where the large Paisleys are shown against both sprigged and striped backgrounds. In the case of Plate 54 one border is set against two different centre infills. Presumably the customer could express a preference for one or the other. The use of diagonal shading to give the effect of twill weave has already been mentioned. Several of the Plates show this particularly well, including numbers 2b, 45, 40a, 52a, 74 and 2a. Plate 11 shows one further technique employed when designing for printed shawls. The drawloom produces a very toothy, angular pattern, rather than the smooth curves that could be achieved on the Jacquard. Sometimes, therefore, if the designer wished to hark back to the days of the drawloom, he would deliberately produce a jagged design to give an air of old-fashioned familiarity to the resultant printed shawl.

Examples of the designers' detailed drawings for different pattern elements are easily discernible. Plate 5 is a corner motif. Four of these would be placed in the corners of the plain area bounded by the patterned borders. This is a pattern layout borrowed directly from the original Kashmir shawls imported during the first decade of the nineteenth century. It proved popular and was frequently used over the next fifty years. Three medallion corners are illustrated in Plates 4a, 4b and 97. The latter is a fairly conventional mosaic of floral elements, the other two are much more geometrical in form. Plate 4b is particularly interesting, since for once the medallion motif is not seen in isolation, but in conjunction with the border of the shawl and the background infill of the centre area. Plate 32a is the finished artwork for a printing block, but a block with a difference. In this case the block is curved and is intended for printing a special variety of shawl known as the 'Glasgow Shawl'. These were usually of the silk-gauze type but instead of being rectangular, they took the form of a huge flattened semi-circle. This was folded at the centre to form a quarter circle, and then again so that the pointed corner draped over the curved edge giving a very pleasing effect. Printing by roller rather than by block was introduced probably around 1860 and designs intended for transfer to rollers can readily be distinguished. The patterns are usually restricted to very small repeats of no more than a few inches. Particularly good examples of this kind of design can be seen in Plates 13, 33, 52a, 70a and 86.

The Plates also show some of the many different kinds of patterns which were popular at different periods during the history of the shawl. For instance, the catalogue of the Great Exhibition held at Crystal Palace in 1851 illustrates shawls of a particular type of design which has almost a feel of the jungle to it. Many foliar Paisleys and other lush vegetal motifs can be seen. Sometimes realistic flowers also occur in these designs. Typical of this style are Plates 8a, 45, 75 and 74b. Dating from the same period there was a short-lived style known as 'Fanny's Fern', seen in Plate 64a.

A much earlier style of design is known as the 'Harlequin' because the patterning is superimposed over large blocks of different colours. Plates 22a, 22b, 24a and 24b are all borders in this style. Also from the early period we find shawls with widely spaced motifs in the form of extremely stylized flowers, as in Plates 6b, 78a and 78b. A motif that was borrowed from Kashmir-made shawls, but used at all periods, was the 'hooked vine'. This is usually used as a linking pattern between the Paisley motifs and can be seen particularly well in Plates 42a and 52a. In Plate 71 it occurs as an extension of the Paisley motif itself. It is also seen in Plate 42b, but this design is more remarkable for the way in which the Paisley motif resembles a fish, a phenomenon which occasionally occurs. Individual large Paisley motifs were always popular on the shawls and several of these designs can be seen, particularly in Plates 23, 42a and 96a.

Occasionally fashionable taste rejected the purely abstract, and at these times designers would include copious amounts of realistic flowers in a bid to win approval from the customers. Roses were by far the most popular and occur in virtually every shawl which exhibits these realistic flowers, as can be seen in Plates 29, 32b, 26b, 55, 56a, 38b, 63, 58a and 60b. Other flowers are also to be found, sometimes recognizable like the blue cornflower in Plate 56a, but at other times difficult to identify. More unusual are the very lifelike ivy leaves in Plate 63.

The use of a tartan effect as a background, as in Plates 21 and 56a, must have been experimental, for despite numbers of these designs occurring in the pattern books there is no actual example of such a shawl amongst the eight hundred or more shawls in the Paisley Museum collection. Last, but not least, the pattern books include many oddities, some of which look as if they could never have been part of a shawl design, such as Plates 7, 25 and 64b. These three appear more like the designs used on printed cottons after World War Two, but are definitely parts of the books which have been in the Museum for many years. Some designs for printed headsquares from the period immediately after shawl production do occur amongst the collection and Plate 35, with its figure-of-eight designs, and Plate 36b, with its circular motifs, may belong to this category.

The pattern books are preserved at Paisley Museum not only as an archive of the history of Paisley's industry, but also as a research tool for the present and the future. Since the shawl itself went out of fashion in the 1870s, the Paisley pattern has never really disappeared. It has always survived in some form. One of the first companies to recognize its potential was Liberty of London, founded in 1875. The archive of their design department shows that Paisley-type patterns were amongst the earliest of the firm's products. Today, of course, Paisley is one of their mainstays and during 1988 the firm acknowledged this with a Paisley promotion of retail goods, coupled with an exhibition of more than twenty original shawls borrowed from the Museum.

Paisley has been more or less fashionable for the last decade but there was a particular upsurge of interest over the 1988–9 winter season. Suddenly not just the Paisley pattern, but the modern version of the Paisley shawl, hit the High Streets of Britain with a vengeance. Virtually all of these modern shawls have the pattern printed on and are mainly produced in Italy. However, they can be found in all qualities, ranging from the very high-class printed silks retailed under couture names such as Hermes and Valentino sometimes costing hundreds of pounds, down to the cheap polyester fabrics which can be bought in any shopping centre. Many of the producers of these modern shawls have consulted the pattern books in the Paisley Museum and have used them as a basis for new interpretations of the ancient motif. The modern shawls differ quite considerably from those worn in Victorian times which were large, heavy and unwieldy (trying to put on a Paisley plaid gives one an insight into the necessity of having a lady's maid!). Today's shawls do not have to cover enormous crinoline skirts or perform the function of a coat. They are often more decorative than practical – in fact, they are usually draped over the wearer's outdoor coat, so they do not need to be as warm as the originals. Consequently they are lighter in weight and much smaller: on average today's shawls measure about 1.3m square. Obviously, therefore, the designs can in no way match the grand scale achieved in the nineteenth century. In fact amongst the shawls currently on the market, the commonest type which is reminiscent of the antique product has a plain colour centre and a sophisticated, almost miniaturized, version of the Paisley plaid designs around the edges. These cheap and cheerful wraps can be found in any and every colour to match any modern outfit.

Today, of course, the Paisley pattern is not confined to the shawl, but may appear anywhere. This trend began in the late 1960s when Paisley was fashionable amongst the Carnaby Street generation. Men's shirts, ladies' jumpers, children's raincoats, curtains and bedspreads were amongst the many textiles to sport the familiar pattern. But increasingly it also began to creep out of the drapers and into other aspects of everyday life, until it found its way onto washbags, mugs, magazine racks, linoleum, pans and carpets, amongst many other things. Eventually the 1960s craze for Paisley died away and the pattern retreated to its usual position on men's ties and pyjamas. However, during this latest period of interest, the pattern has again adorned a multitude of household objects. Recent months have seen Paisley patterned wallpaper, memo pads, vases, photograph frames, curtains, diaries, writing paper, trays, ceramic tiles, oven gloves, photograph albums and make-up. These words have even been written with a Paisley patterned ball-point pen! The possibilities seem to be endless.

Valerie Reilly
Keeper of Textiles and Local History
The Paisley Museum and Art Gallery
Paisley, Scotland

The Plates

PLATE 1

*An unusual design strongly featuring
stylized floral motifs, which come from the
volume entitled* Early Harness Sketches,
1823–1843.

PLATE 2a

This design for a printed shawl, complete with 'twill' lines, is of the sort of repeating design associated with roller printing.

PLATE 2b

This pattern clearly shows why, in some parts of Europe, the Paisley motif was referred to as the 'tadpole'. It is also a good example of the diagonal lines incorporated in order to give the effect of the woven fabric.

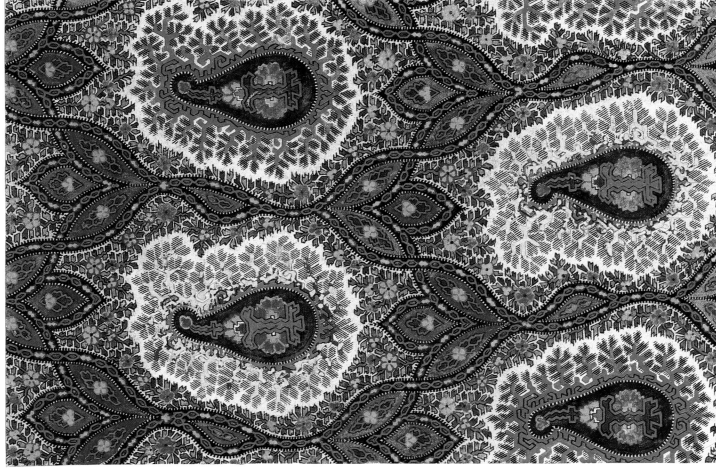

PLATE 3

*Printed shawl design with unusual 'toothy'
edged Paisley motif, which comes from a
volume of* Sketches for Print Shawls,
English and French, *c.*1850.

PLATE 4a

Design, c.1830, for a medallion centre shawl.
It could be used as drawn for the corners of
the shawl, or multiplied fourfold for the
central pattern.

PLATE 4b

Design for a very geometrical medallion
corner, which also shows the borders and
part of the centre pattern. It probably dates
to c.1830.

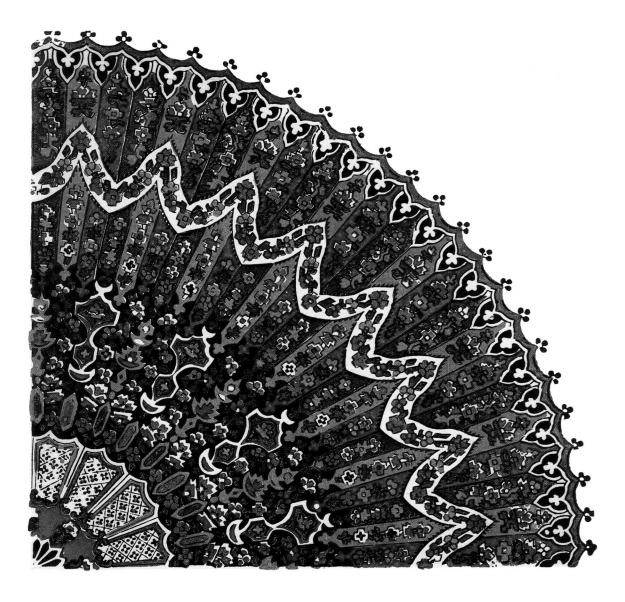

PLATE 5

This corner motif of the 1840s comes from a volume of print designs enigmatically entitled No 2. *An inscription reads '2 blotches £9–8'. Presumably this was the cost of the having the blocks cut.*

PLATE 6a

From a selection of **Early Prints 1840–1845**
*comes this pull from a block. It exhibits the
tendency for early print designs to recall the
woven shawl designs of some thirty years
before.*

PLATE 6b

1820s design featuring stylized floral motifs.

PLATE 7

An odd, simplistic Paisley design, perhaps intended for roller printing. It is shown in two colour combinations.

PLATE 8a

*Design very much in the style of the shawls
exhibited at Crystal Palace in 1851.*

PLATE 8b

*This design for a printed shawl (note the
'twill weave-effect' line) is stamped as being
the work of George Haite of London. Other
examples of his work are known from the
Victoria and Albert Museum.*

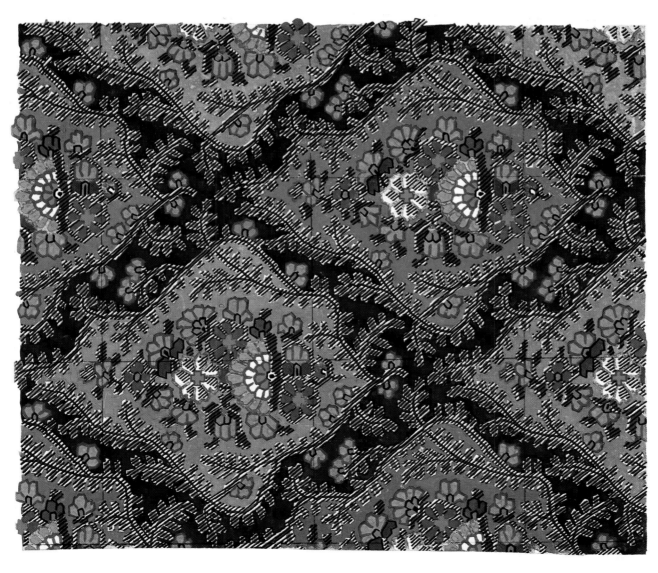

PLATE 9

*Drawing on the squared-off paper, this
design shows the stylized floral style.*

PLATE 10a

From the folder entitled 'Pulls for Paisley Patterns', this is a typical design for roller printing.

PLATE 10b

This simple design appears to be intended for roller printing.

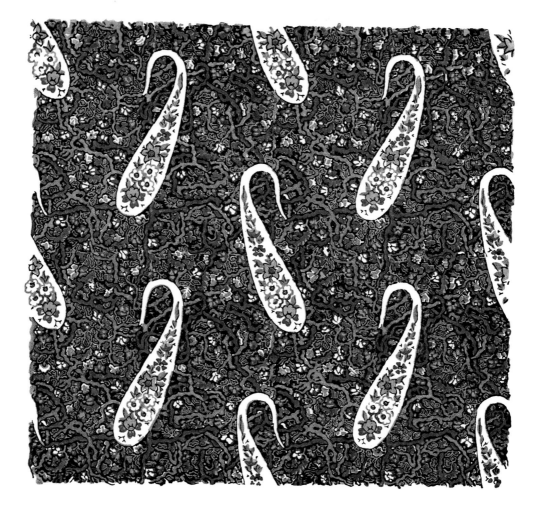

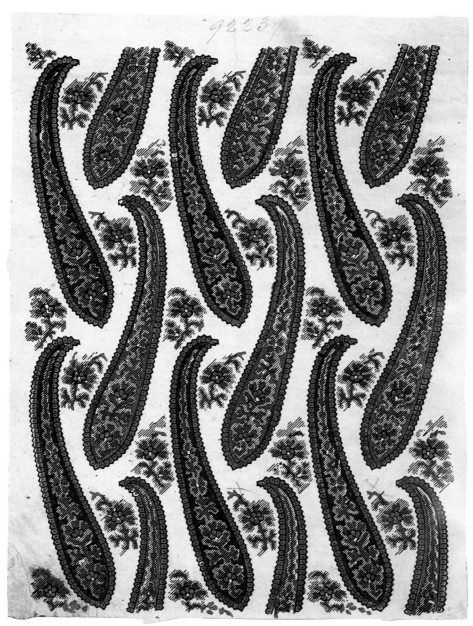

PLATE 11

Small-scale design probably intended for roller printing.

PLATE 12a

This Yuill and Houston registered design of 1875 lists twelve different colour variations.

PLATE 12b

A printed sprig from the volume of Yuill and Houston's registered designs of 1857. The book shows five colour variations for this pattern, and also details of a matching border.

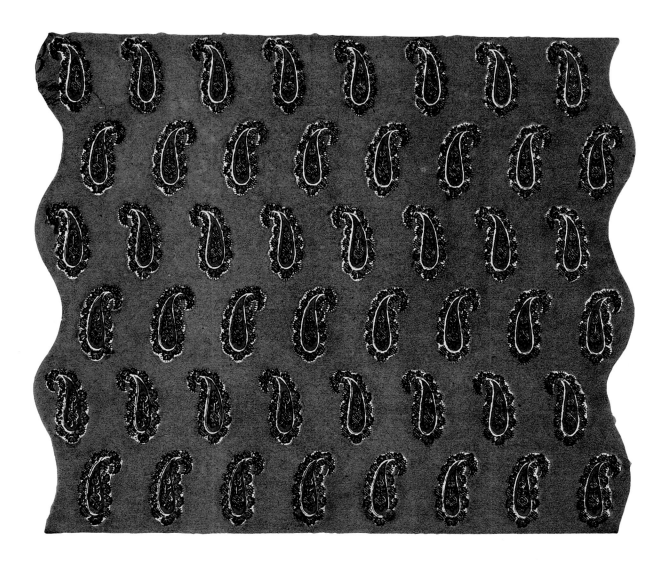

Nº 23

PLATE 13

A border design in an interesting variation of the 'Harlequin' style. Probably dates to c.1830.

PLATE 14a

*From the unnamed book of French and
English design the gauze prints of the 1850s.
This is a design for the edge of an imitation
plaid.*

PLATE 14b

*From Print Sketches c.1857 comes this
sophisticated design, where three small
Paisley motifs are constrained within an
oval.*

PLATE 15

This gauze print pattern carries the stamp of the designer, 'Chles Boucherat, Paris, 7 Rue Mazagran, Boule. Bonne Nouvelle'. It dates to the 1850s.

PLATE 16a

*An unusual striped design for a silk gauze
printed shawl c.1860.*

PLATE 16b

*A striped design for a gauze print perhaps
intended for roller printing.*

PLATE 17

Sometimes the outline of the Paisley motif was made, not so much by its filling, as by the absence of the pattern immediately around it. This design gives a particularly good example of the 'voided' technique.

PLATE 18

These two patterns from the book of Designs for Gauze Prints, French and English, 1850–1860, *show us that the sprig design of the central area was called filling, whilst the border design was called the flounce.*

PLATE 19

An early border pattern of extremely stylized floral motifs.

PLATE 20a

A fine printed shawl design, probably intended for roller printing, presented to the Museum by former shawl manufacturer John Robertson.

PLATE 20b

1860s' design for a silk gauze printed shawl.

PLATE 21

This seemingly most Scottish of designs, with its tartan background, is actually stamped 'J. Huntington, Dessinateur, Paris'.

PLATE 22a

An 1820s' border design in 'Harlequin' style.

PLATE 22b

A 'Harlequin' border in which the Paisley motifs are alternated with an unusual kind of sunburst design.

PLATE 23

*This Paisley motif, with its leafy appendage
so reminiscent of the Great Exhibition style,
actually comes from a folder of sketches for
print shawls dated 1851, the year in which
the Exhibition took place.*

PLATE 24a

An example of 'Harlequin' style border.

PLATE 24b

Small Paisley motifs on blocks of different colour background go to make up this 'Harlequin' style border design.

PLATE 25

In this pattern the designer J. Huntington of Paris, has experimented with alternative background for the large Paisley motifs.

PLATE 26a

Design for a silk gauze printed shawl c.1860.

PLATE 26b

This gauze print shawl design is executed on tissue and has unusual realistic flowers forming part of the central sprig design.

PLATE 27

*A gauze print design of the 1850s, with
beautiful sprays of tiny flowers separating
the Paisley motifs.*

PLATE 28a

The gauze print design c.1850 stamped 'J. Huntingdon, Dessinateur, Paris'.

PLATE 28b

A delightful small-scale border design from pattern book of Print Designs 1853–1860, *which was donated to the Museum in 1941 by one of the last of the Paisley textile manufacturers.*

PLATE 29

This individual motif is taken from a book put together by an unknown manufacturer of Gauze Print Designs, French and English, 1850–1860. *It is certain that this is not a scrapbook, but did belong to one manufacturer, because throughout, in the same hand, are instructions for which machine was to be used for each design. This pattern was destined for 'No. 1 machine'.*

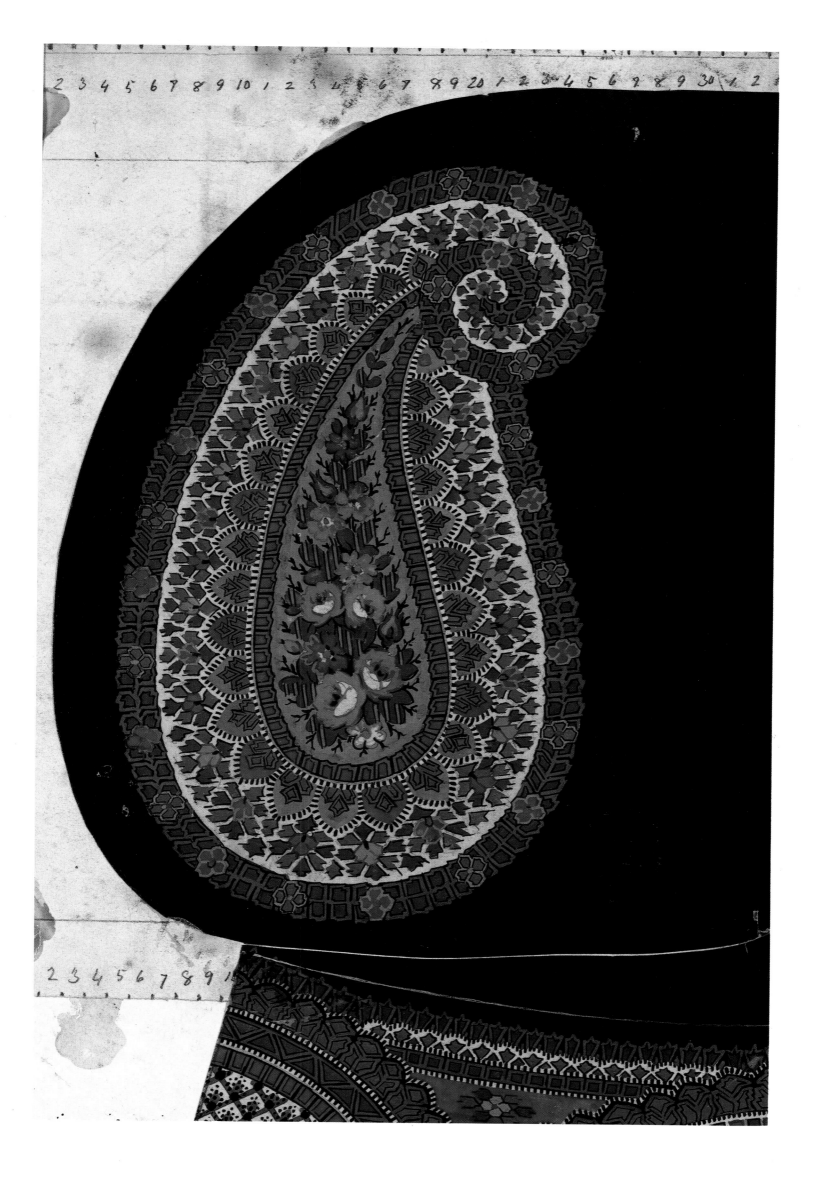

PLATE 30a

Design for a printed shawl, painted on tissue paper. It may have been intended for roller printing.

PLATE 30b

Design c.1855 for a printed shawl, probably a silk gauze.

PLATE 31

A border design in an untypically subdued
colour scheme. It probably dates to the 1830s.

PLATE 32a

*Design for the border of a gauze print shawl.
It was drawn by J. Huntington, perhaps in
Paris, but has been overstamped with his
London address of Queen's Road Works,
Holloway. It is a curved edge block for a
'Glasgow Shawl'.*

PLATE 32b

*This small pattern is from the volume entitled
'Designs for Gauze Prints, French and
English, 1850–1860'.*

PLATE 33

*This design, on its red background, comes
from a folder of 'Pulls from Paisley Patterns'.*

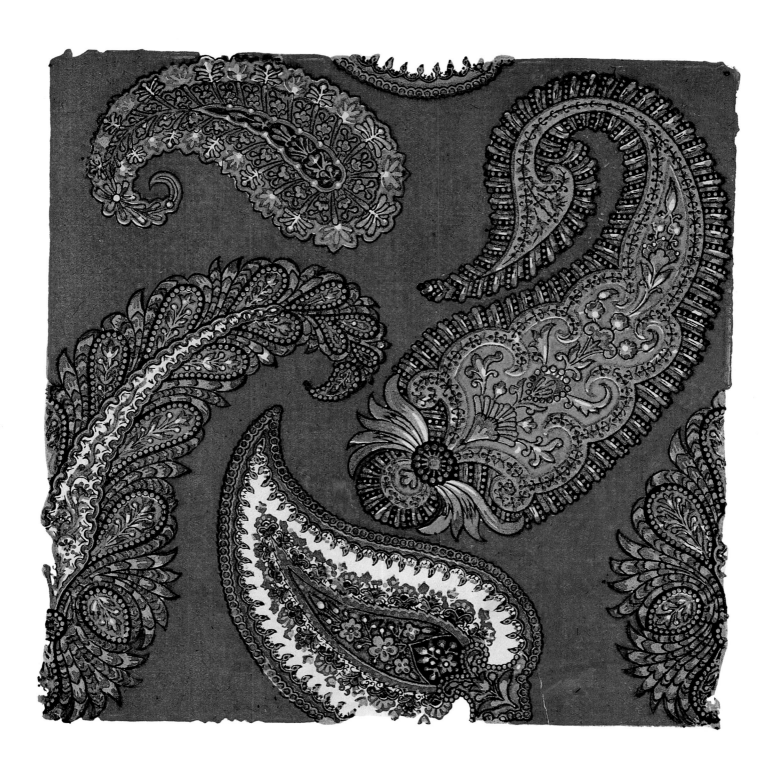

PLATE 34a

*A very delicate design for a gauze print
shawl of the 1850s, which an inscription
states 'needs 13 repeats for the filling'.*

PLATE 34b

*This gauze print design shows the effect that
different colour backgrounds can give.*

PLATE 35

This very unusual design is possibly for a headsquare rather than a shawl, and may be post 1870 in date.

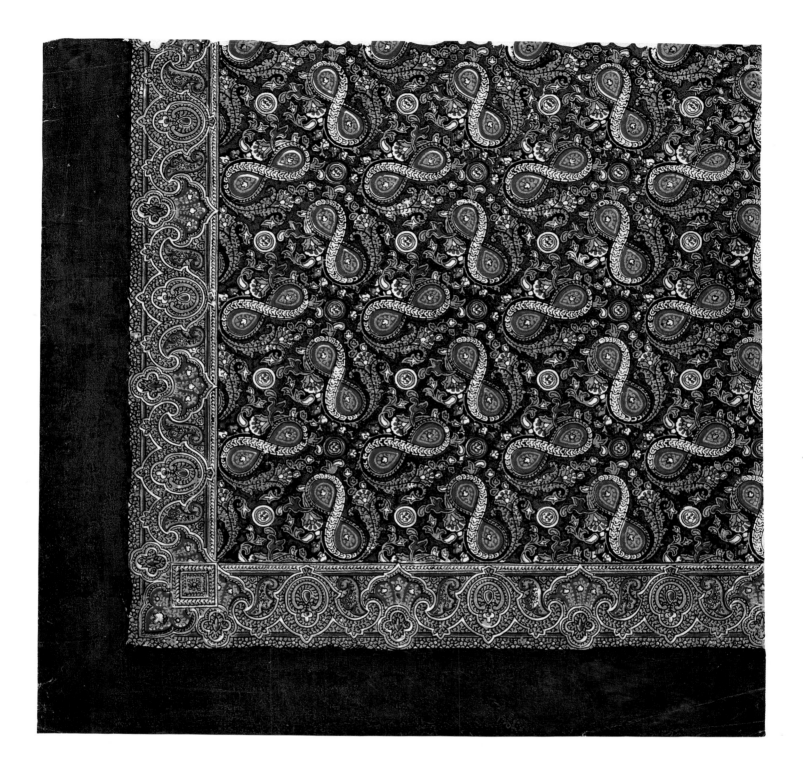

PLATE 36a

*This pattern shows unusually elongated
motifs, almost reminiscent of birds' beaks.*

PLATE 36b

*A most unusual design of circular motifs
which may be intended for a* post 1870s'
head square.

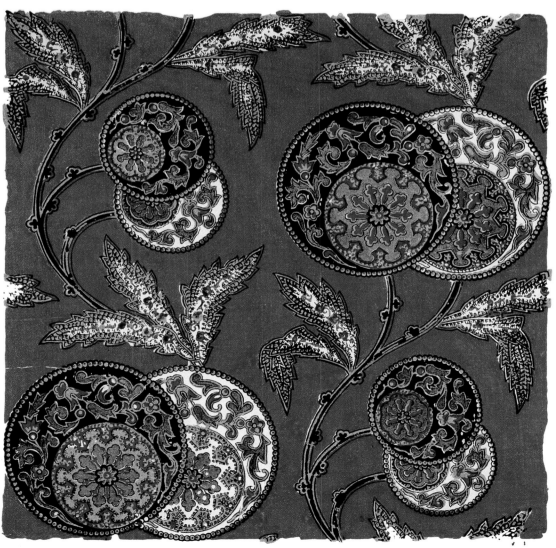

PLATE 37

*This design is typical of the 1840s, making
use of the Indian fan motif and the leafy
shapes. Also of interest is the small motif at
the left completely infilled with stripes.*

PLATE 38a

1840s' design with odd elongated Paisley. A strange combination of geometric infill on one motif and realistic flowers on the other.

PLATE 38b

It is noted that this 1850s' design for a printed imitation of a Kirking shawl would require three colours.

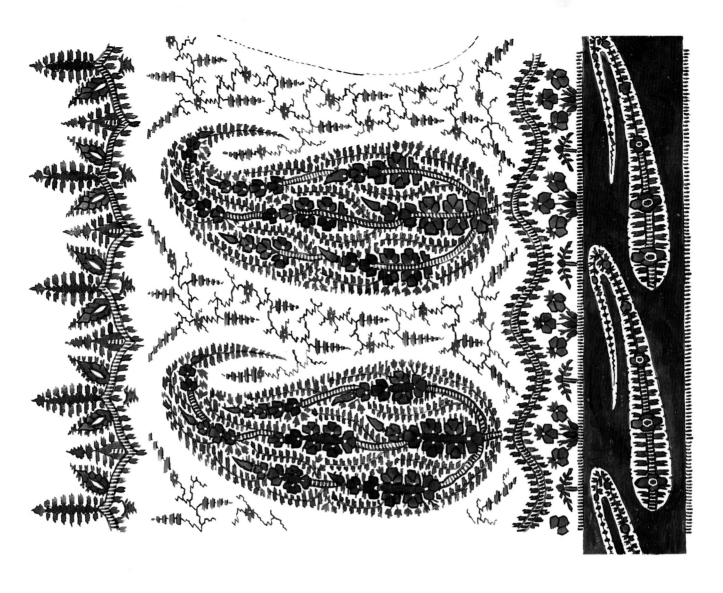

PLATE 39

This typical 1840s' motif is part of a pattern which also includes floral tendrils linking together various parts of the design.

PLATE 40a

*A design for a printed shawl, executed by
George Haite, probably in the 1850s.*

PLATE 40b

*A design taken from a book of manufacturers
Yuill and Houston's registered designs of
1857. It is for a 'Glasgow Shawl' as there is a
drawing for a matching curved block.*

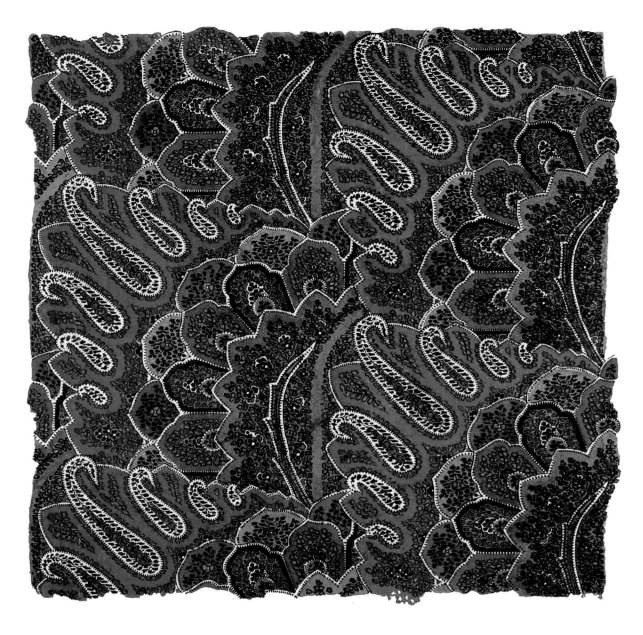

PLATE 41

This very unusual design comes from a book that also contains some of the most conventional paisley designs. It probably dates to c.1860.

PLATE 42a

*An 1840s' border design with fine large
Paisley motifs linked by hooked vines. The
colours of the pattern are particularly
vibrant.*

PLATE 42b

*A design of the 1840s' which features the
hooked vine motif, and Paisley motifs which
closely resemble a fish.*

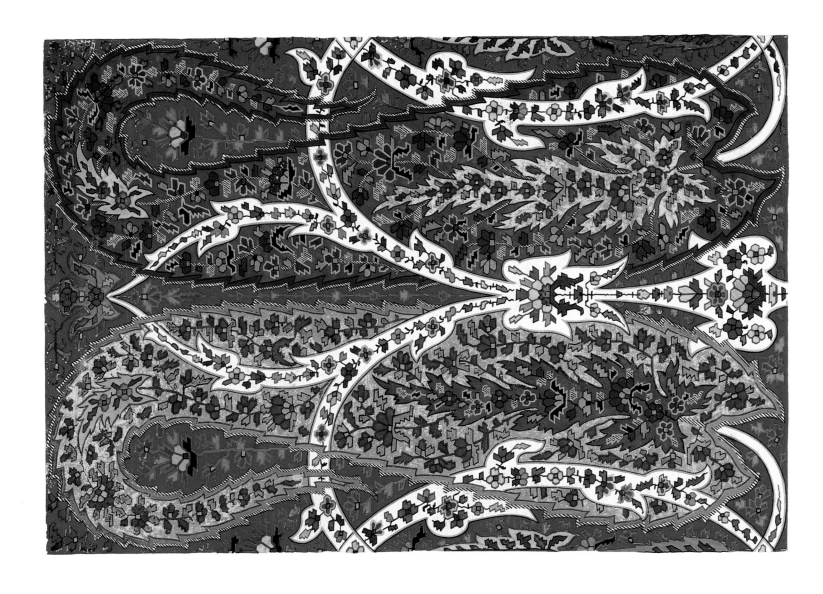

PLATE 43

This fine border of the 1840s' period comes from a volume entitled Shawls Sketches, English and French, 1845–1850.

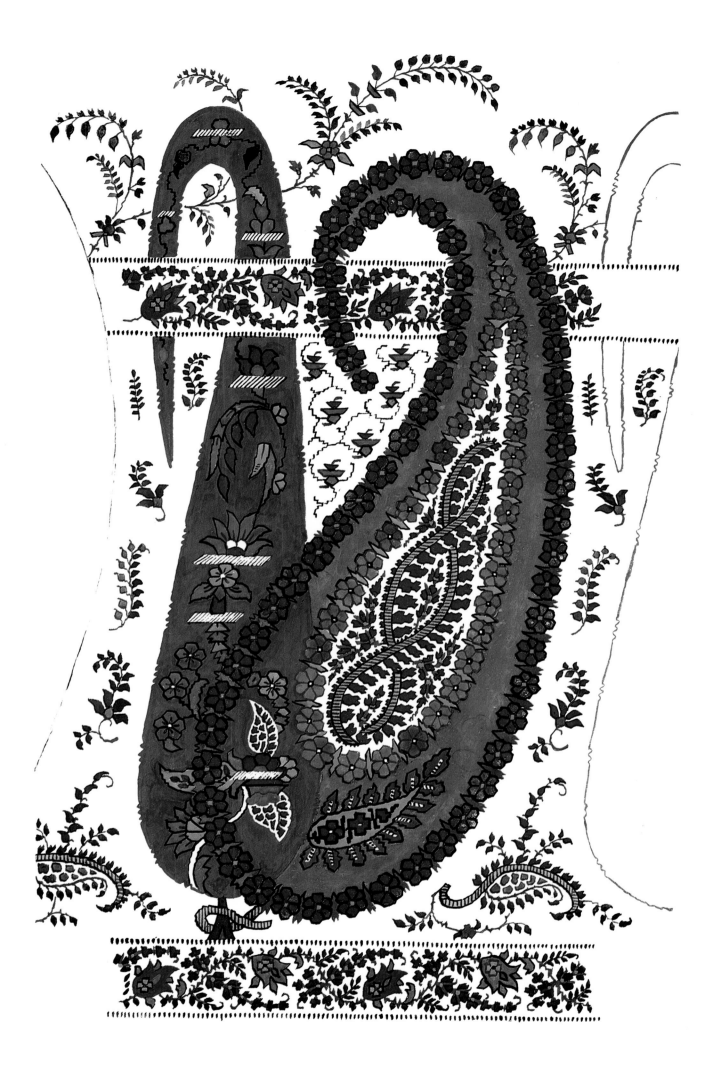

PLATE 44a

This design appears to be by the same hand as Plate 38b, but instead of requiring three colours, it has only two. It comes from the volume of Shawls Sketches, English and French, 1845–1850.

PLATE 44b

An 1840s' border design for a printed imitation Kirking shawl.

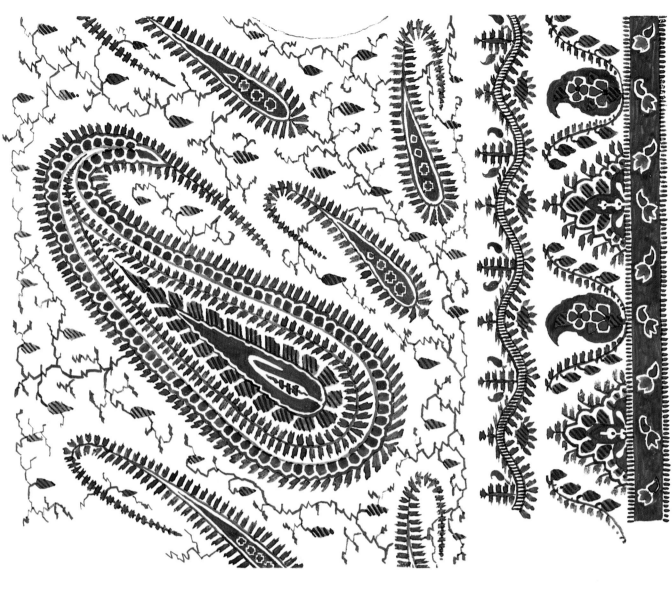

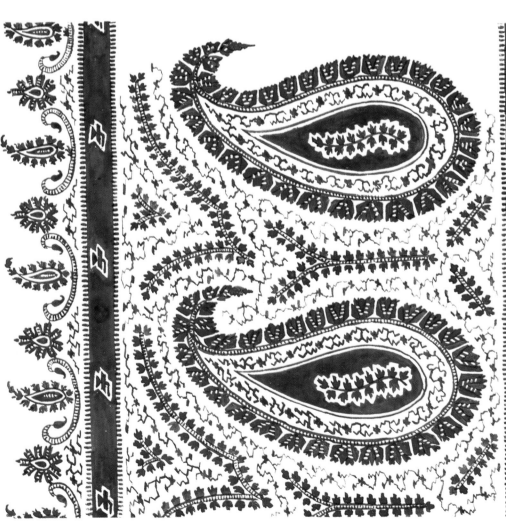

PLATE 45

This George Haite (1845–1871) design is one of the best examples of the use of diagonal lines to give the effect of woven fabric. It is also an archetypcal specimen of the Great Exhibition style.

PLATE 46a

This single large motif probably dates from about 1850 and would have been intended for a Kirking shawl. It is an example of a voided motif, where the outline is delineated by an absence of background infill.

PLATE 46b

A border detail. Part of a series of designs presented to Paisley Museum, at the beginning of the twentieth century, by John Robertson, a former shawl manufacturer.

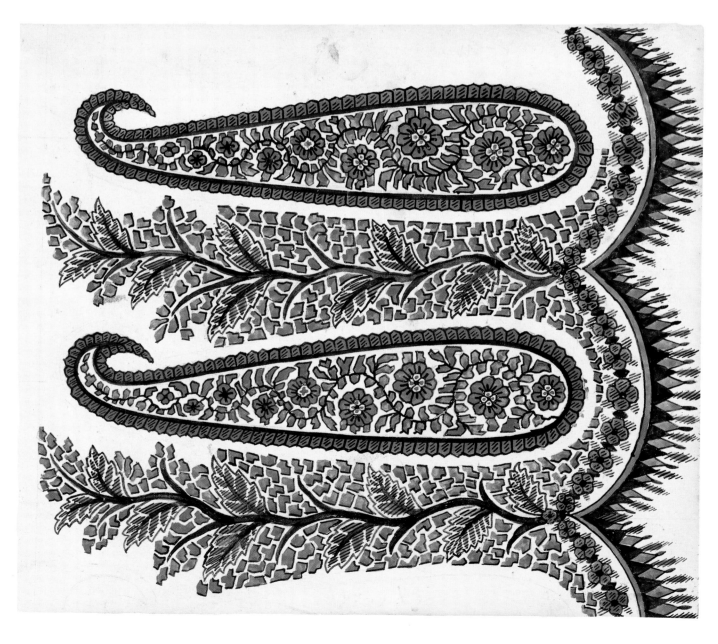

PLATE 47

Border design of the 1850s, executed on tissue.

PLATE 48a

An 1840s' shawl design with a striped border and a central area of small Paisley, linked by a twig pattern.

PLATE 48b

This colourful design comes from Shawl Sketches, English and French, 1845–1850.

PLATE 49

An intriguing design in which the Paisley motifs seem to be superimposed on a cell-like structure. A limited repeat which would be ideal for roller printing. Dates to c.1860.

PLATE 50a

Print Sketches c.1857 includes this strange, almost chintzy, design.

PLATE 50b

Designs for printed shawls, like this 1850s' example, often record earlier styles. This appears to be a reworking of the 1820s' 'Harlequin' idea, with motifs on blocks of different coloured backgrounds.

PLATE 51

*An unusual design for printed shawls which
combines several different Indian motifs.*

PLATE 52a

From a volume of designs, presented to the Museum by former shawl manufacturer, John Robertson, comes this Paisley and hooked vine pattern which appears to be intended for roller printing.

PLATE 52b

This small-scale design, with its un-Paisley-like diamong shapes and floral infill, actually came to the Museum from formal shawl manufacturer John Robertson.

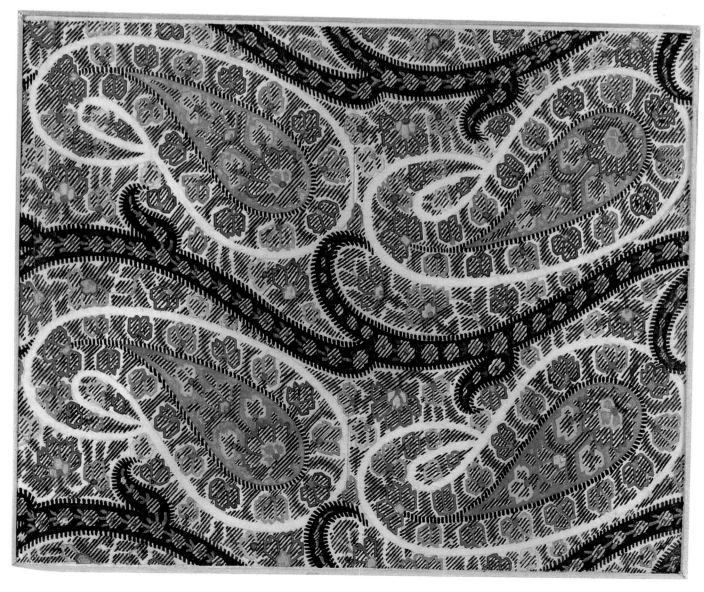

PLATE 53

This painted design comes from a volume of Sketches for Printed Shawls, English and French, *c.1850. It is stamped, 'Carter, Hyland, Hudson and Purnell, Designers, Paris and London'.*

PLATE 54a and b

Two very odd designs executed in sepia tones and making extensive use of realistic leaf shapes. They date to the 1850s.

PLATE 55

A sophisticated design of c.1860 which includes very realistic roses among the more abstract florals.

PLATE 56a

*An 1850s' border design, featuring realistic
flowers over a tartan background.*

PLATE 56b

*A very geometric border design for an 1840s'
gauze print shawl.*

PLATE 57

A small, delicate, striped design where, unusually, one stripe of pattern seems to be superimposed over the other.

PLATE 58a

A border design of floral swags from the volume of Designs for Gauze Prints, French and English, 1850–1860.

PLATE 58b

Taken from Designs for Gauze Prints, French and English, 1850–1860, *this pattern, with its realistic roses, was to be set on No. 1 machine, according to the inscription.*

PLATE 59

A striped design, very similar in style to Plates 16a and 16b, is stamped by 'Chles Boucherat, Paris, 7 Rue Mazagran'.

PLATE 60a

A J. Huntington design, from his London works, for border on a gauze print shawl.

PLATE 60b

A sophisticated floral and geometric design c.1860, which is stamped 'J. Huntington, Queen's Road Words, Holloway, London'. Like most of the designs featured it is inscribed with both its number from Huntington's portfolio, and the number allocated to it by the unknown Paisley manufacturer.

PLATE 61

*A beautiful design of intertwining Paisley
shapes and hooked vines dating from the
1840s.*

PLATE 62a

An elegant, pastel-coloured design for a gauze print shawl of the 1850s.

PLATE 62b

A gauze print shawl design stamped 'J. Huntington, Dessinateur, Paris'.

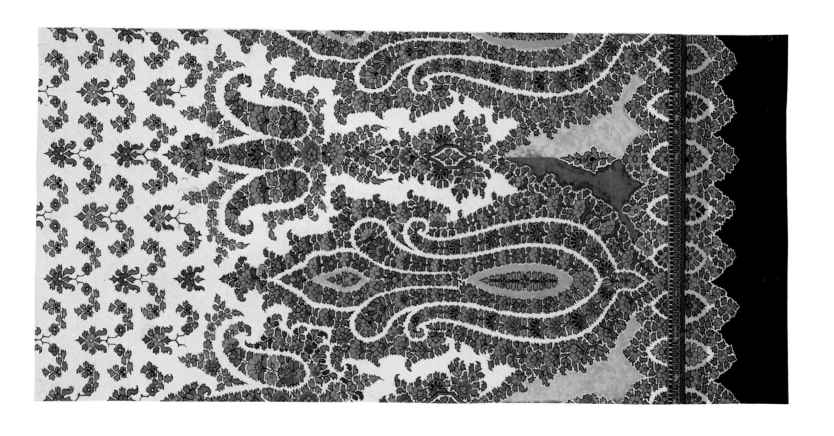

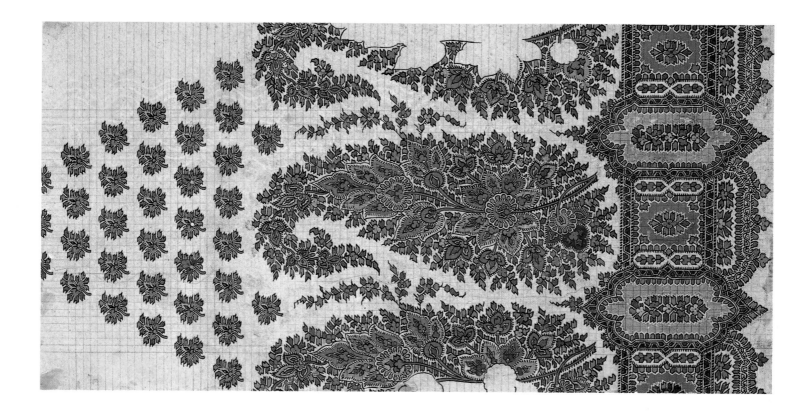

PLATE 63

This 1850s' gauze print border design
features both realistic roses and ivy leaves.

PLATE 64a

A border for a shawl designed in the 'Fanny's Fern' style. It dates to the early 1850s.

PLATE 64b

This extremely odd design is accompanied in the book with samples of printed material, proving that it was actually produced.

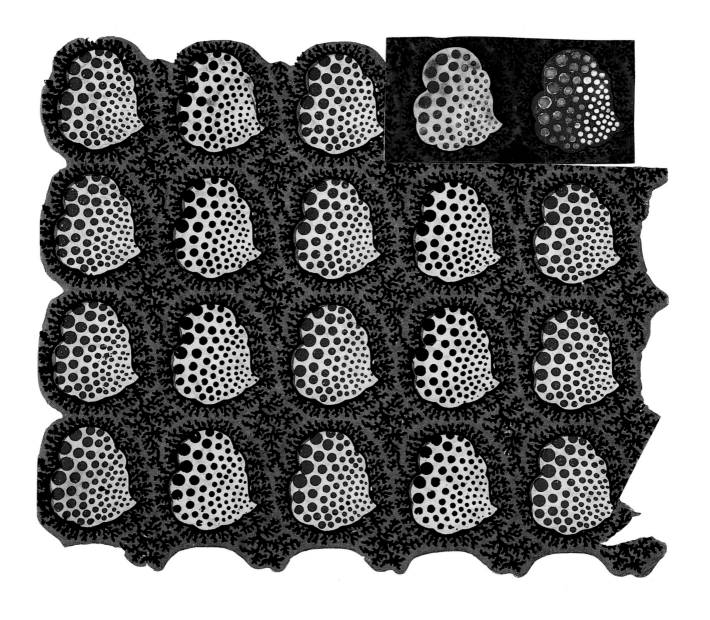

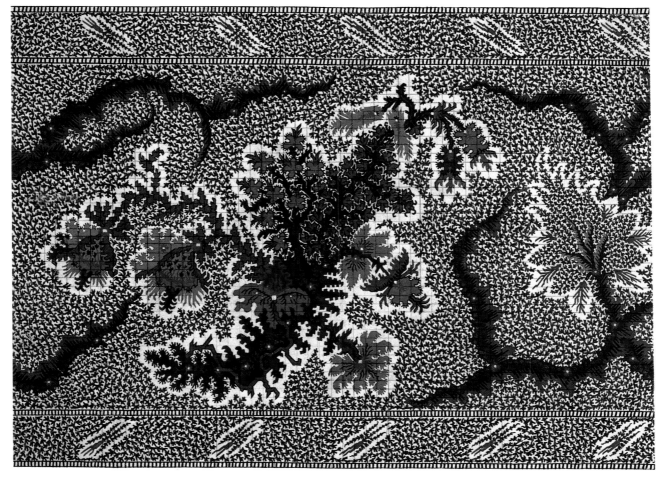

PLATE 65

An 1850s' finished artwork for a printing block.

PLATE 66a

*A very beautiful border design with 'voided'
Paisley infilled, and standing out from a
scatter of stylized flowers. It is from the
volume of* Shawl Sketches, English and
French, 1845–1850, *but is very much in the
style of the 1820s.*

PLATE 66b

*This delightful French design of the 1840s is
stamped 'Wetler and Hubner, 3 Rue St Roch,
Paris'.*

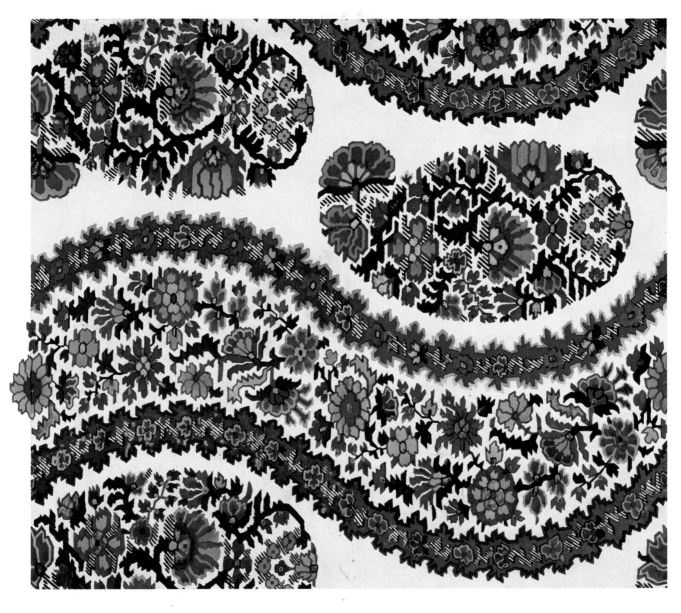

PLATE 67

*This motif was invented for a printed shawl
as can be seen by the weave-effect lines. It
probably dates to the 1860s.*

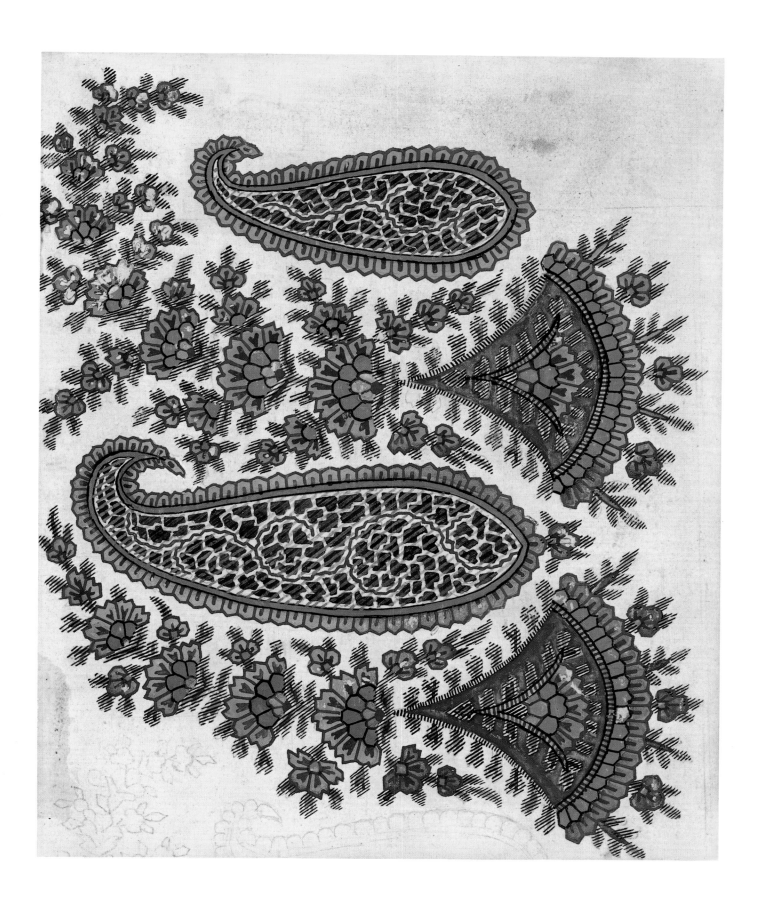

PLATE 68a

*Design for an 1840s' printed shawl showing
weave-effect lines.*

PLATE 68b

From the volume entitled Shawl Sketches,
English and French, 1845–1850, *this
unusual design has the tail of the motif
extending beyond the confines of the borders,
and also the strange posy of stylized flowers
over the motifs.*

PLATE 69

A beautifully constructed, voided Paisley motif drawn on oil-paper. It probably dates to the 1850s.

PLATE 70a

An unusual design for roller printing, which looks more like upholstery fabric than a Paisley shawl.

PLATE 70b

From amongst the designs presented by John Robertson comes this sketch for roll printing.

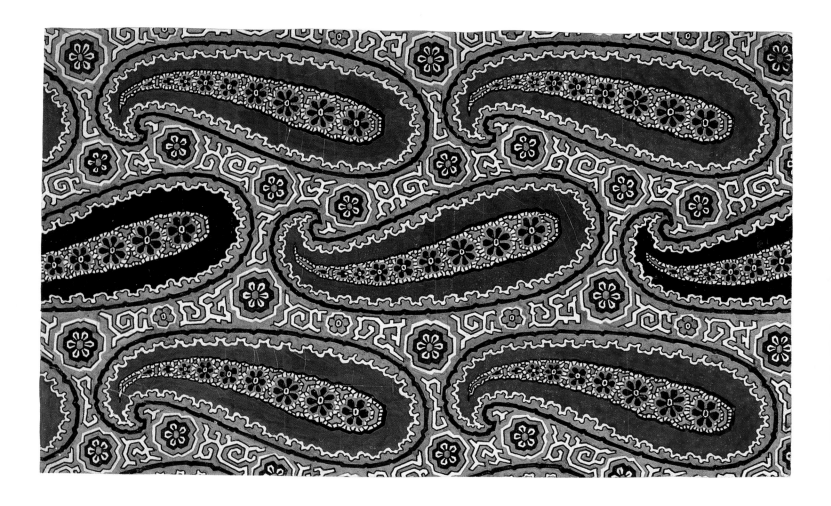

PLATE 71

This design, where the hooked vine appears to grow out of the Paisley motif seems to exhibit the same cell-like background structure as Plate 61.

PLATE 72a

A design for printed materials which has a look of weeping willow trees.

PLATE 72b

From a folder of Sketches for Printed Materials *c.1860 comes this extraordinary design with a motif disguising a change of background colour.*

PLATE 73

*This design is difficult to date because of its
odd blend of sophistication of outline, and
naïveté of infill pattern.*

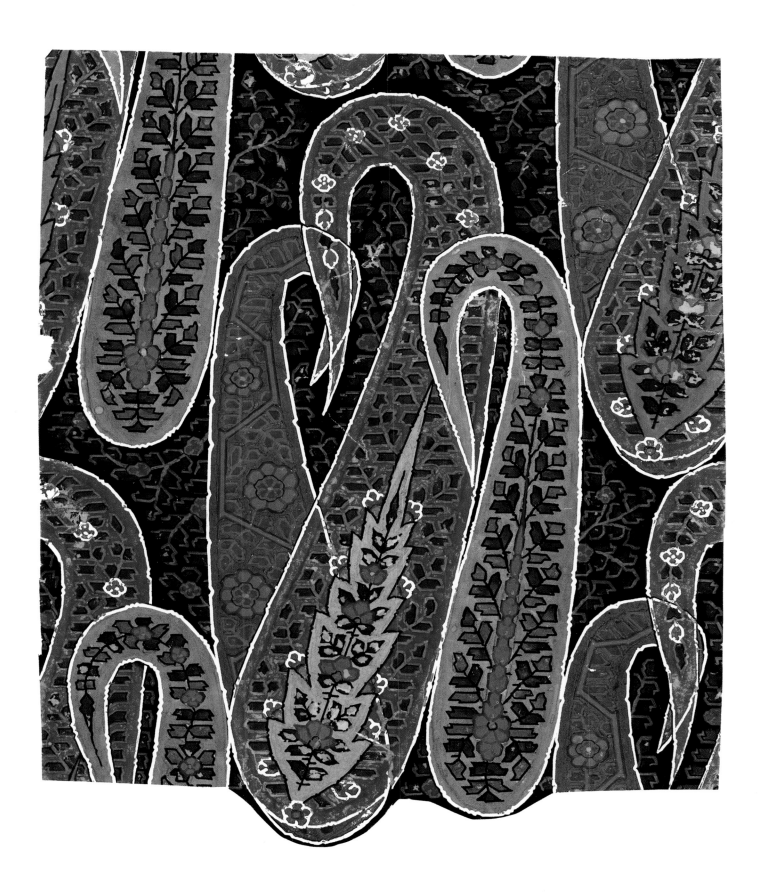

PLATE 74a

*This printed material design c.1860, could
have been intended for roller printing with
its small pattern repeat.*

PLATE 74b

*This design for printed material is thought to
be c.1860, but is in fact very reminiscent of
the designs from the Great Exhibition period
nearly ten years earlier.*

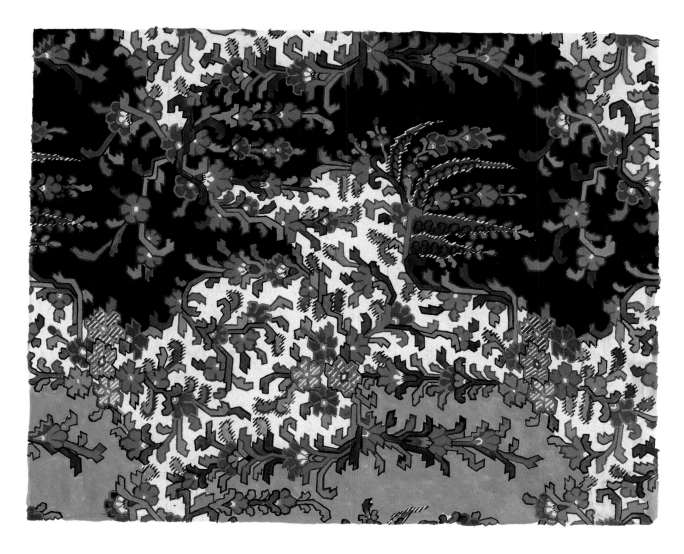

PLATE 75

Design for a printed shawl, showing the
vegetal style familiar from the catalogue of
the Crystal Palace Exhibition of 1851.

PLATE 76a

The 1840s saw the advent of what had been called the 'Yardage Shawl', where great lengths of shawl were woven with a small repeating pattern. Shawl sizes were then cut from the cloth, and finished off with ready-made fringing sewn all round. This particular design is perfect for that sort of shawl production.

PLATE 76b

A delicate design taken from a volume of Shawl Sketches, English and French, 1845–1850.

PLATE 77

*An interesting design for a striped shawl
where exactly the same stylized motif is
superimposed over each colour background.*

PLATE 78a

A stylized flower design of the mid 1840s which may have been intended for Yardage shawls.

PLATE 78b

This Yardage shawl design, instead of being floral, has a fishy Paisley motif.

PLATE 79

A typical design for an 1840s shawl, with a floral Paisley and stylized flower superimposed over a striped background.

PLATE 80a

A fine border design, with a brilliant electric blue used to great effect on a black background. The Paisley motifs are voided from the surrounding pattern.

PLATE 80b

A spectacular design with almost dayglow colours set against a black background. From the intertwining form of the main motif it appears to date from the 1840s.

PLATE 81

This design is inscribed 'Runner 1200 plaid, 700 type, 14/8/49 A.P.

PLATE 82a and b

Small repeat designs of the 1860s for roller printing.

PLATE 83

*Design for a printed shawl of the early 1850s
from the volume presented by former shawl
manufacturer John Robertson.*

PLATE 84a

Design for a printed shawl with a striped border, and a tiny Paisley motif forming the infilling of the centre area. It probably dates to the 1850s.

PLATE 84b

Design for a printed shawl of the 1850s, unusual for its subdued colour scheme.

PLATE 85

Finished artwork for a printing block of the 1850s. Part of the collection presented by John Robertson.

PLATE 86a and b

Two sophisticated 1860s' designs, both of which are suitable for roller printing.

PLATE 87

The finished artwork for a printing block of the 1850s. The small motif sticking out to one side would facilitate registration during the printing process.

PLATE 88a

This design for a gauze print had an actual sample of the material alongside it in the book.

PLATE 88b

A pull from a printing block for a gauze print shawl c.1860.

PLATE 89

An unusual design with small, angular, geometric Paisley, set with squares and bounded by floral borders. It dates to the late 1840s.

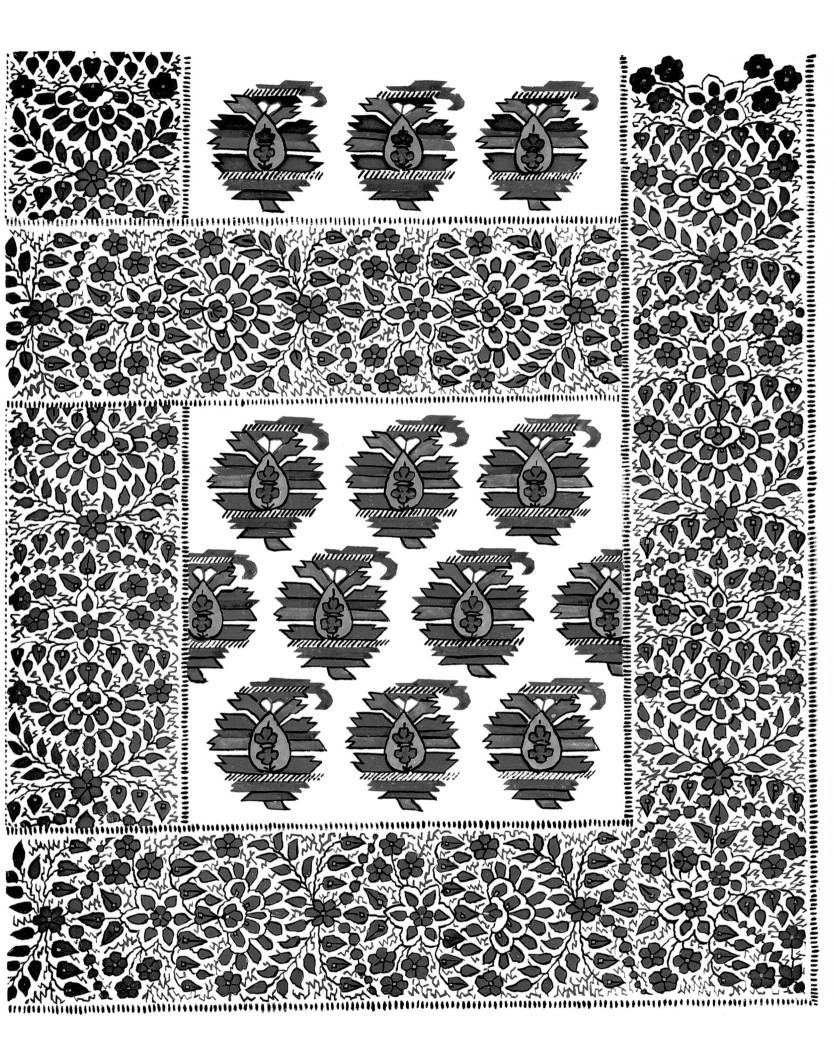

PLATE 90a and b

Small-scale design from a volume of Shawl
and Border Designs 1844.

PLATE 91

A border design of intertwining floral
Paisleys from the volume of Shawl
Sketches, English and French, 1845–1850.

PLATE 92a

Realistic flowers and leaf motifs separate the green and black background areas of this printed material.

PLATE 92b

This design, with its green and black background colours, is from the folder Sketches for Printed materials *c.* 1860.

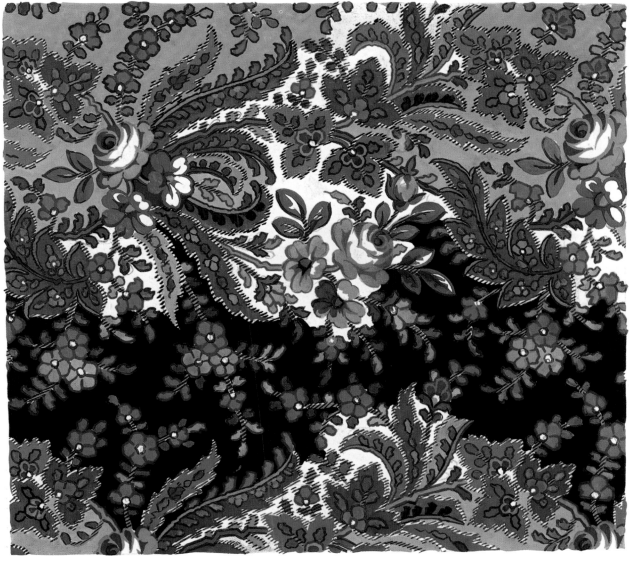

PLATE 93

*Finished artwork for a printing block of
1840s' date.*

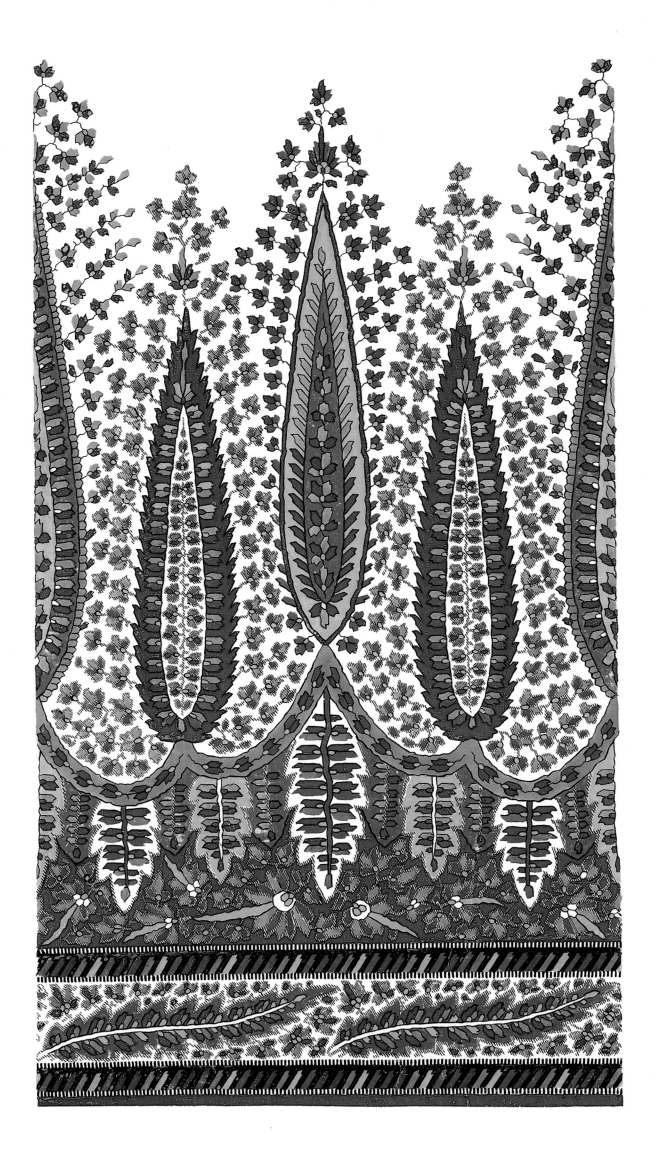

PLATE 94a

*An unusual design, with flowers growing
from two thorny branches, wrapped around
with a floral ribbon.*

PLATE 94b

*This 1860s' design for printed material could
equally well be adapted for a striped shawl.*

PLATE 95

Border design with Paisley motif of bright blue colour, voided from a black background.

PLATE 96a

A stunning Paisley border motif from the volume of Early Harness Sketches, 1823–1843.

PLATE 96b

This leafy border design is from a volume of Early Harness Sketches, 1823–1843, *and is thought to be an 1830s' design from the manufacturing of W. & H. Provan, George Street, Paisley.*

PLATE 97

This medallion design, with its infilling of stylized flowers, probably dates to the 1820s.

PLATE 98a and b

Examples of very geometric style border
patterns drawn in 1844.

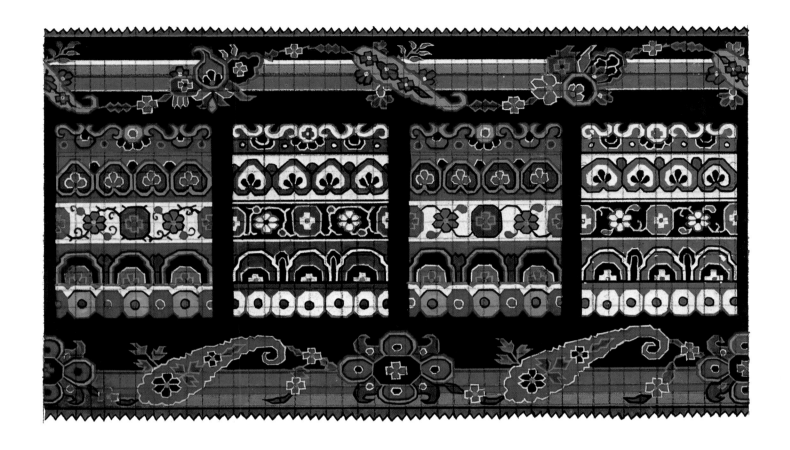

PLATE 99

Design for printed material c.1860, showing
'weave-effect' lines.

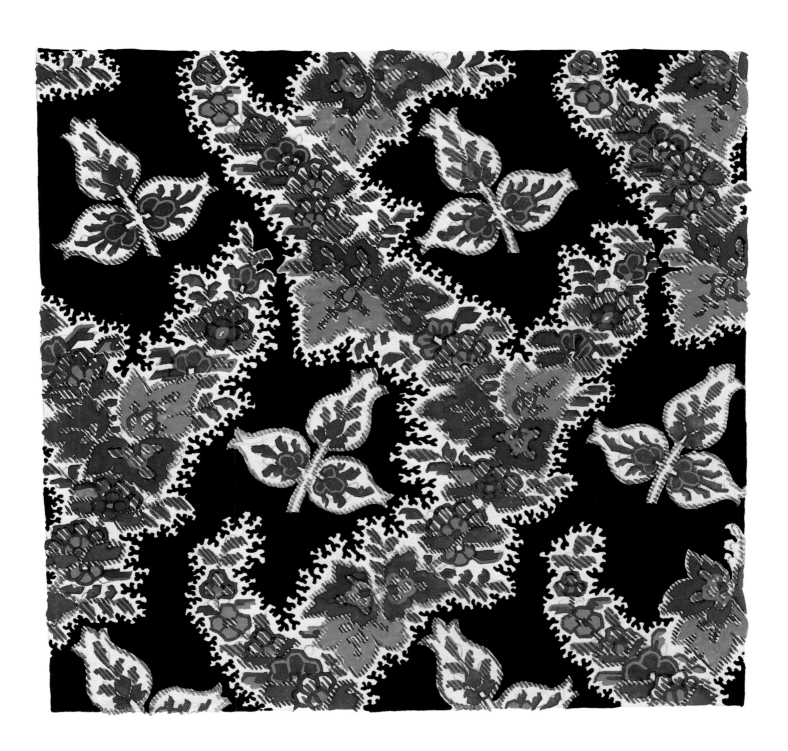

PLATE 100a

Border design reminiscent of the 'Fanny's Fern' style of the 1850s.

PLATE 100b

Very early border design, possibly pre-1820, featuring leaf and floral motifs.